DITCH THE MOMMY GUILT

DITCH THE MOMMY GUILT

A BLUEPRINT FOR THE MODERN MOMMY

DR. LEESHA M. ELLIS-COX

purposely
created
PUBLISHING

DITCH THE MOMMY GUILT
Published by Purposely Created Publishing Group™
Copyright © 2018 Leesha Ellis-Cox

Printed in the United States of America
ISBN: 978-1-948400-70-1

DEDICATION

To Bailey, Evan, and Khloe: my three heartbeats, my beautiful children who ushered me into motherhood.

To my love, my husband, Kenneth: thank you for bringing balance and order to my chaos, gut-busting laughter to my days, and earnest prayers to my tears. Thank you for loving me through my own struggles with mommy guilt.

And to all the mommies, new and seasoned, who question every parenting decision, who wonder if this thing called motherhood will ever get any easier, or whose hearts ache from unrelenting guilt, overwhelming pressure, and a pervasive sense of dread that their best is simply not good enough: this book is for *you*! You are enough!

TABLE OF CONTENTS

INTRODUCTION

"There will be so many times you feel like
you've failed, but in the eyes, heart, and mind of your
child, you are super mom."

—Stephanie Precourt

I'm a forty-plus-year-old woman, a board-certified child, adolescent, and adult psychiatrist, a wife of over fifteen years, and a mother to three young children. I know a little "somethin' somethin'" about parenting. Over the last several years, I have experienced tremendous joy, as well as many difficult challenges, in my personal life and similarly have witnessed such ups and downs in the lives of the thousands of children and families whom I have had the honor and privilege to serve. Building upon the richness of these experiences, I have formulated a few quips related to life, love and marriage, and parenting that I frequently share with family, friends, patients, and now my readers.

The following sayings reflect my attitudes, beliefs, and intentionality as a woman who fulfills several roles for many—a manifesto of sorts to beautifully guide me through life with grace, humor, and practicality:

1. The two hardest (and arguably two most important) things I will ever accomplish in my life are to stay married and raise my children.

2. Our children often thrive in spite of us.

3. Laughter is good for the soul.

4. Smiles are contagious: give them freely and generously.

Moms, I hope you will truly enjoy this book and that the words and stories contained within it will inspire you, encourage you, and remind you that you are enough!

CHAPTER 1

INFANTS, CHILDREN, AND TEENS: THEY DON'T COME WITH INSTRUCTION MANUALS

*"The moment a child is born, the mother is also born.
She never existed before. The woman existed, but
the mother, never. A mother is something absolutely new."*

—Rajneesh

Nothing about my foray into motherhood was easy or predictable. I vividly recall the day I found out that I was pregnant with our first child, Bailey. It was exhilarating, and I couldn't wait to share the news with my husband, sister, and parents.

The road to getting pregnant had been much less exciting for me. While my pregnancy was planned, getting pregnant required much more "work" than I expected. Our first attempts quickly went from fun to frustrating as pregnancy test after pregnancy test came up negative. As close friends shared their pregnancy news, despair started to creep in. My husband and I decided to switch from a "natural" path to a more scientific one: an ovulation kit. Yes, even a physician needs help to accurately determine her own ovulation schedule! But soon, with the help of the kit, "voila" we were pregnant.

Despite all my medical school education, I was ill-prepared for what transpired next. A few days before I was scheduled to fly to New York City to sit for my general psychiatry oral board examination, I started to experience abdominal cramps. I was just shy of twenty-four weeks and proud of my protuberant belly. The sudden tightening threw me for a loop. Hoping the cramping would let up, I didn't freak out right away; but my anxiety grew as it continued.

My husband was busy at work and unavailable, so I called my neighbor. He graciously agreed to take me to the hospital. There, my worst fears materialized. I discovered that I was in premature labor and would have to be hospitalized to stop the labor. Those next seventy-two hours were some of the scariest of my life. I thought I might lose my precious baby girl. During my stay, I was diagnosed with cervical insufficiency, also termed an incompetent cervix, which happens when the cervix spontaneously thins and opens prematurely during pregnancy. Cervical incompetence is one of the leading causes of second-trimester pregnancy loss.

Following my hospital discharge, I spent fourteen weeks on strict bed rest. I literally could only go up and down the stairs once per day and could only stand or walk to use the bathroom and bathe. Otherwise, I was to remain off my feet, lying on my left side. I alternated between seeing my regular OB and maternal fetal medicine specialist on a weekly basis. My only saving graces were the distraction of planning my sister's wedding and my dear friend Ruth who brought me thrilling conversation, lunch, and a movie every week until Bailey made her debut.

My first pregnancy was nothing like I expected. I had all these grand ideas—cute maternity dresses, maternity photos, and seeing family and friends "ooh and ah" as my baby bump grew— but all that was replaced with bed rest, Heparin injections to prevent blood clots, and anxiously counting down the days and weeks. Every week she stayed put meant a lower risk of preterm birth and its associated complications.

At my thirty-seven-week appointment, I was already dilated four centimeters and Bailey's growth had slowed. My obstetrician was worried that she might have intra-uterine growth restriction (IUGR), a serious condition in which a baby's growth in the womb is abnormally slow and puts her at risk for certain health problems such as hypoglycemia (low blood sugar) and difficulty maintaining body temperature. I would have to give birth *that day* to prevent further complications. I was frantic. It was too early and she was too small! My knowledge as a physician only made matters worse. All we could do was pray that Bailey would be all right.

It bears repeating: my foray into motherhood was neither easy nor predictable. Still, Bailey arrived four weeks early, weighing only 5 lbs. and 8 oz., but healthy and beautiful. We were completely enamored and utterly in love.

Even as memories of my unexpected pregnancy complications faded and joy and gratitude filled my life, I again found myself unprepared—this time for mother-hood. Everyone, from other parents to friends to plain old strangers, has parenting advice. There are literally thousands of books and websites. I was told what to do, what not to do, and everything in between, which left me confused and overwhelmed. I desperately wanted to be the most amazing mommy to ever grace the earth.

I knew I had to breastfeed because, well, we all know that "breast is best." I took breastfeeding classes, purchased a baby scale to measure Bailey's weight before and after nursing so I could adequately determine how many ounces she'd eaten, and hired a lactation consultant. Bailey was also only going to have organic, homemade pureed baby foods, so I purchased a snazzy baby food processor. My baby was going to be on an airtight feeding and sleeping schedule. Plus, I was going to lose my baby weight quickly since I was breastfeeding.

Um, so yeah, none of this happened. I was completely drained. Despite several visits to the lactation consultant, Bailey had fundamental trouble latching, which led to sore, cracked nipples and a bout of mastitis. I tried to pump more frequently but did not produce a lot of milk. On top of this, I had the baby blues. I was moody, irritable, and felt like the biggest fraud. This smart and capable physician mommy couldn't even nurse her daughter right! With tears running down my cheeks, I begged my mom to stay with me as she prepared to return home.

Two weeks just wasn't enough. I needed her longer. I just didn't see how I was going to survive without help.

I had no idea that having a newborn would be *this* hard. Even if people had warned me beforehand, I wouldn't have believed them. There is really no way to prepare for motherhood other than to simply go through it. Those first two to three months kicked my butt. I was mentally and physically exhausted. Even the idea of returning to work seemed like a fabulous vacation to Fiji compared to staying home with a crying baby who ripped my nipples to shreds every time she nursed.

I needed guidance, a "So, You're a Mommy Now" boot camp. But soon I realized that, while there is a lot of good information out there, no one has the magic formula for your unique personality that fits with your lifestyle and your baby's temperament. You must figure it out for yourself through trial and error. That's why my pregnancy and childbirth experiences with baby #2 and baby #3 were better. I already knew the pregnancy complications I would face and could anticipate some of the concerns I might have.

Even still, each baby brings his or her own personality. Life perpetually changes and children grow. Each age our children enter heralds a different developmental stage. As a child and adolescent psychiatrist, I'm intimately familiar with these developmental stages and the various theories of child development that inform these benchmarks. Some of these theories have been and continue to be enormously helpful to strategically tailoring my parenting game. They improve my understanding of my children's basic needs, as well as their primary developmental tasks and level of cognitive functioning at various stages.

While there are many theories that have been opined, my two favorites are psychologist Erik Erikson's theory of psychosocial developmental and psychologist Jean Piaget's cognitive developmental theory. Both are detailed below.

TABLE 1
ERIKSON'S THEORY OF PSYCHOSOCIAL DEVELOPMENT

AGE	STAGE	BASIC TENETS
0 – 1	**Trust vs. Mistrust**	**Infant:** New to the world, a baby knows very little about his environment. He relies on his mother (primary caregiver) to meet his basic needs, create a loving and nurturing space, and maintain stability and consistency. He learns to *trust* his mom and develops a healthy attachment or he becomes insecure and apprehensive when care/parenting is inconsistent and unpredictable (*mistrust*) **Dr. Leesha's Parenting Pearl for *Trust vs. Mistrust*:** Meet your baby's needs. Hold him. Rock him. Sing to her. Respond to her tears and her laughter. Earn his trust. There is no such thing as spoiling a baby.

AGE	STAGE	BASIC TENETS
1 – 3	**Autonomy vs. Shame or Doubt**	**Toddler:** At this stage, toddlers become increasingly mobile and verbal, which brings about a strong desire for independence. She is walking, feeding herself, making choices about what she wants to do and what she chooses to wear, and is toilet training. She is developing a strong sense of self-control.
		Parents must encourage and support their toddler's need for independence, allow him to explore his world and make choices, and give her the freedom to make mistakes without criticism or tight control (*autonomy*). When parents are too restrictive and criticize their toddler's failure rather than extolling praise for even the smallest of developmental feats, they foster dependence, risk crippling his self-esteem, and create a sense of doubt.
		Dr. Leesha's Parenting Pearl for *Autonomy vs. Shame or Doubt*: Nurture your toddler's independence. When she proudly shouts, "No, mommy, I can do it," by all means, let her.

AGE	STAGE	BASIC TENETS
3 – 5	**Initiative vs. Guilt**	**Preschooler:** Cooperative play (playing with others) and forming friendships are critical developmental tasks for preschoolers. The child learns to play with peers at school, strengthens her social skills as she interacts with others, and increases her assertiveness as she initiates games and various activities with friends. During this process, she may play appropriately with her friends or become too forceful and overbearing. Parents must help their children find balance within those peer interactions by giving them the space to successfully negotiate their decisions and relationships (initiative). If parents interrupt that process and become overly involved or punitive, they effectively inhibit these skills, which can lead to guilt and stifle creativity. **Dr. Leesha's Parenting Pearl for *Initiative vs. Guilt*:** Encourage your preschooler's creativity, let him make new friends, and don't step in too early when conflict arises.

AGE	STAGE	BASIC TENETS
5 – 12	**Industry vs. Inferiority**	**School-aged kid:** A child in this developmental stage acquires new skills such as learning to read and write and adding and subtracting, among others. Mastery of these skills boosts his self-esteem and self-confidence (*industry*), and makes him feel capable of setting and achieving his goals as he demonstrates competency.
		When parents push their children too hard to master specific skills or even discourage them from attempting challenging tasks, they may cause their children to question their abilities or feel incompetent.
		Dr. Leesha's Parenting Pearl for *Industry vs. Inferiority*: Mistakes happen. Teach your children to learn from their mistakes, champion their attempts at mastery, and help them find new strategies rather than belittling their failed trials or suggesting they avoid challenges altogether.

AGE	STAGE	BASIC TENETS
12 – 18	Identity vs. Role Confusion	**Adolescent/Teenager:** This period reflects a time of transition—shifting from childhood to adulthood and all that being a "grown-up" encompasses. The primary developmental task for a teenager is to cultivate her sense of personal identity, which includes ideas about sexuality and gender roles, educational and career goals, religious beliefs, and political affiliations. Undergirding this is a tremendous desire for social acceptance and inclusion. When parents give adolescents the opportunity to safely explore their ideas and beliefs with some guidelines and boundaries in place, these young people begin to successfully formulate their identity. Without this, teens will become confused and lack clarity about their role on both individual and societal levels. **Dr. Leesha's Parenting Pearl for _Identity vs. Role Confusion_:** Despite the inherent turmoil that is adolescence, celebrate your teen's transition into adulthood. Keep lines of communication open and judgment free where appropriate. Encourage questions and answer honestly—but that doesn't mean divulging _all_ the dirty details.

AGE	STAGE	BASIC TENETS
18 – 40	Intimacy vs. Isolation	**Young adulthood:** At this stage, young adults desire to develop and maintain committed and loving relationships outside of family (intimacy). Without such relationships, they often feel isolated and lonely.
		Dr. Leesha's Parenting Pearl for *Intimacy vs. Isolation*: Your child is now an adult, so respect their desire to connect with others on a much deeper level.
40 – 65	Generativity vs. Stagnation	**Middle age:** Men and women in this stage have attained certain goals—established families, cultivated their careers, and actively engaged within their communities (church, civic organizations, volunteer efforts). They are no longer focused primarily on themselves as individuals but have, instead, adopted a broad concern for their family and society in general (*generativity*). If these primary tasks are not met, middle-aged adults feel unproductive and stagnant.

AGE	STAGE	BASIC TENETS
65+	**Integrity vs. Despair**	**Elderly:** These adults are now considered elderly, often seen as "old" by most standards. Typically, these adults have retired from their jobs/careers, their children are grown and have families of their own, and their day-to-day activities have slowed down. In the latter stages of life, individuals find themselves reflecting on things of the past. Are they personally fulfilled? Have they lived a rich and full life? Have they realized their dreams (*integrity*)? During this time, some struggle to accept the inevitability of death or find themselves dissatisfied with the life they created (*despair*).

TABLE 2

PIAGET'S COGNITIVE DEVELOPMENTAL THEORY

AGE	STAGE	BASIC TENETS
0 – 2	**Sensori-motor**	At this stage, infants and toddlers are just beginning to interact with and explore the world through their five senses—seeing, hearing, smelling, tasting, and touching. They start to walk and to talk and to learn through trial and error.
		Object permanence, the ability to recognize that something still exists even when it is no longer in sight, is the primary developmental task during this stage. For example, a toddler will know that a red bouncy ball that rolls underneath the sofa is still present and retrievable even when it is no longer visible to the child.
		Dr. Leesha's Parenting Pearl for the *Sensorimotor Stage*: Our babies are learning and growing at an incredible rate. They use their senses to learn through trial and error. Be patient.

AGE	STAGE	BASIC TENETS
2 – 7	**Preopera-tional**	Within the preoperational stage, children have improved language skills and engage in imaginary play and make-believe. *Symbolic thinking*, which is seen in drawing, writing, speaking, and pretend play, occurs when words, symbols, or internal images represent objects, persons, and events that are not actually present.
		Another hallmark of this stage is *egocentrism* wherein children believe the world revolves around them and they struggle to see things from another's perspective.
		Dr. Leesha's Parenting Pearl for the *Preoperational Stage*: Our children truly believe they are the center of attention. Recognizing this should lessen your frustration when they seem to only care about themselves—their self-centeredness is developmentally appropriate. And play is critical so go ahead and affix your pretend crown, don your fancy dress, and enjoy tea and scones with the queen of the house.

AGE	STAGE	BASIC TENETS
7 – 11	Concrete Operational	Entering the concrete operational stage signals the beginning of *logical thinking*. Now, children can solve problems in their head rather than through trial and error. They can group objects that share similarities like shape and color, a skill known as *classification*. They also learn to conserve measures such as mass and weight which means they understand that quantity remains the same even when appearance changes, such as three different sized vases that all contain the same amount of water (*conservation*). **Dr. Leesha's Parenting Pearl for the *Concrete Operational Stage*:** Children are making sense of their environment during this stage. They continue to grow and learn. Help them think through problems when they arise. Strengthen their logical thinking skills.
11 – Adulthood	Formal Operational	For the formal operational stage of cognitive development, youth are more future-oriented, begin to test hypotheses and use predictions when answering questions, and employ abstract thinking. **Dr. Leesha's Parenting Pearl for the *Formal Operational Stage*:** Continue to help kids think through difficulties as they occur and apply logical strategies to address them. Encourage them to anticipate and prepare for their future.

EXERCISE #1
I IF I HAD ONLY KNOWN THEN WHAT I KNOW NOW

Write down five things you wish you had known before you started a family. Then write what you have learned since raising your children.

What I wish I knew

1) _____

_____

2) _____

_____

3) _____

_____

4) _____

_____

5) _____

_____

What I have since learned

1) _____

_____

2) _____

_____

3) _____

_____

4) _____

_____

5) _____

_____

CHAPTER 2

IN THE BEGINNING: ORIGINS OF THE DREADED MOMMY GUILT

*"When you're in the thick of raising your kids…
you tend to keep a running list of everything you think
you're doing wrong."*

—Connie Schultz

I didn't hear the term "mommy guilt" until I was well into parenthood, but I remember experiencing the guilt almost immediately. I felt inadequate for several reasons. I had a lot of trouble breastfeeding and wanted to quit, but I knew that both the American Academy of Pediatrics and the American College of Obstetrics and Gynecology recommended exclusively breastfeeding for at least the first six months. I also didn't want my mom to leave me alone by myself to take care of my baby, which made me feel weak and ashamed. While my other friends and physician colleagues had planned a three-month maternity leave, I wanted to return to work so badly and that, too, made me feel horrible. I kept thinking that every mom knows how to instinctively care for her baby. I mean, women have been giving birth and caring for children since Adam and Eve. So why wasn't I figuring this thing out?

The day that really broke me was about seven years ago. Bailey was three, and she and her toddler classmates had put together a special Mother's Day tea for all the moms. I received a sweet invitation to the program; but with only a few days' notice, I couldn't reschedule my entire afternoon clinic. Regrettably, I made the decision to skip the tea.

When I arrived later that evening to pick her up, Bailey was devastated. Tears filled her eyes, and she softly asked, "Mommy, where were you? Why did you miss the tea?" Instantly, I felt like I had been punched in the gut. I stammered, trying to find the right words to explain to my heartbroken three-year-old why her mommy felt like work and patients were more important than spending the afternoon with her to enjoy tea and cookies. I could barely look her in the face. As tears welled up in my eyes, I grabbed her and hugged her tightly. I proceeded to apologize profusely for my grave mistake. This was the failure of all failures—I had totally botched this parenting thing. I quickly concluded, "I'm a horrible mommy." It seemed like forever before I was able to forgive myself. Even now as I recount that story, some of those same guilty feelings tug at my heart.

Typically, "mommy guilt" is a term ascribed to mothers who work outside of the home, but all mommies experience mommy guilt. There are a myriad of inciting events: deciding to formula-feed instead of breastfeed, taking a trip with just your hubby, calling or not calling the pediatrician when your child gets sick, using technology as a babysitter, getting easily frustrated and yelling, worrying that you don't spend enough attention with your children, failing to read to your children every night, overspending and underspending, having too many or not enough extracurricular activities...the list goes on. There are so many circumstances and choices that dredge up mommy guilt.

Mommy guilt arises from a variety of sources. We, as mothers, tend to place tremendous pressure on ourselves to parent perfectly at all times. Aside from that, our husbands/father of our children, our mothers, our friends, our families, and society as a whole also have expectations for mothers. According to findings from a 2007 national survey conducted by the Pew Research Center[1], 70% of American men and women believe it is more difficult to be a mother now than compared to twenty to thirty years ago, while 60% believe that being a father is more difficult today. Startlingly, 56% say that mothers do a worse job than in the past (compared to 47% for fathers), and *women* were the most critical of today's moms. In fact, 54% of women think that today's mothers perform worse as parents, with the highest rates (66%) being among middle-aged women between ages 50 – 64. It's no wonder women often choose to suffer with mommy guilt in silence: we indeed judge and are judged by other women.

In 2009, there was an interesting paper in *Evolutionary Psychology* by Finnish family sociologists Anna Rotkirch and Kristina Janjunen, entitled "Maternal Guilt."[2] I will summarize a few salient points from the paper here:

1. Concept of the motherhood myth: moms are often described as "universally present, nurturing and kind."

2. Fatigue, love, rage, anger, aggression, and guilt were the five emotions most commonly mentioned by moms in this study, and the negative emotions were perceived by many as "forbidden."

3. They postulated five proximate reasons for mommy guilt.

    a) *Aggression (actual or imagined)*: moms feel incredibly guilty when they yell, call their children names, or have thoughts of physically harming their children such as squeezing, pushing, or slapping them.

    b) *Exit*: moms experience guilt when they think about abandoning their children and family, have thoughts of suicide or self-harm, or wish that their child was never born.

    c) *Absence*: moms feel guilty when they contemplate checking out from their children emotionally and/or physically, such as dropping them off with family for a long weekend or being emotionally unavailable because of marital strife or discord.

    d) *Preferential treatment*: when there are multiple children in the family, moms may prefer one child over another because of the age of the children or their differing temperaments or needs. They feel guilt for not loving their children equally.

e) *Motherhood myth*: the idea of "social disapproval," whether real or imagined. Guilt arises from cultural expectations of mothers and their failure to be perfect, which then puts the child at risk of harm.

The findings in this study of Finnish mothers were eye opening and aptly captured the mommy guilt struggles I face in my own life and discuss with only my closest friends and family. These are the same fears echoed by other moms in my larger circle filled with acquaintances, colleagues, church members, and the moms whose children I treat. We fear that we are bad moms because we yell and scream, can be impatient, and have bad thoughts about our children. We believe that there is only one right way to parent and that failure to adhere to the "right way" means that we inadvertently or intentionally harm our children, leaving them ill-prepared for the future and saddling them with our hurts, hang-ups, and bad habits.

This research study begs the question "How did we get here?" or alternatively, "Why is our identity as women so closely tied to our ability to birth and raise children?" I will not expound upon motherhood through the ages here; but I will say that, since the world began, women have birthed and raised children. Motherhood is expected and virtually required of women. Whether the process of child-rearing occurs in isolation or with significant involvement from dad and the extended family; whether the mother works inside or outside of the home; whether a mother is celebrated and revered or is merely viewed as property—her role and very identity rest within the sociopolitical context of the culture in which she exists.

On top of that, parenting is almost always viewed as the primary responsibility of the mother. We have conjured up this false image of the idealized, romanticized mother who is constantly present and available, joyful, nurturing, patient, self-sacrificing, and graciously willing to put the needs of others, especially those of her children, before her own—an archetype that abounds in Western culture. Every mother who has even one "bad" thought that veers from that ideal is seen as selfish and unfit.

We must do better, moms, and I don't mean by fulfilling that perfect, Stepford wife mold. Striving for perfectionism in parenthood is an unattainable goal with great costs to ourselves, our marriages, our relationships, and especially our children. We are human, and humans make mistakes…sometimes a lot of them. We have erroneously convinced ourselves that perfect mothers raise perfect children even though we know, on some level, that that is so far from the truth. Mommy guilt is good for no one, not yourself or your family.

To quote Elsa from the Disney movie *Frozen*, we must "Let it go!" Let go of the mommy guilt. Otherwise we toil, compare, judge, and pass blame. We hide and secretly agonize over every parenting decision we make and don't make, and bury ourselves in more and more guilt.

Here are five signs that you are struggling with mommy guilt:

1. You wonder how your neighbor's house is always spotless when she has three young children, while your home with only one child is in a perpetual state of clutter.

2. You worry what your mom will say if you ask her to keep your infant for the weekend so you can get some much-needed rest.

3. You panic when you realize you have a meeting for work and will have to ask your significant other to take your child to see the pediatrician for the well-child check.

4. You refuse to attend a breastfeeding group since you don't want to admit that you are supplementing with formula.

5. You rebuke your mom friend who has devised a fun-filled vacation to escape from parenting, but you are secretly jealous that she has the guts to even think of such a trip.

Truthfully, mommy guilt is ubiquitous. I honestly believe all moms will experience some form of it throughout their parenthood journey, though not all to the same degree. Now, guilt is not all bad since it sometimes helps us see that we need some additional help outside of venting to friends. Nevertheless, we cannot pursue the unachievable goal of perfect parenting at the expense of our overall health and well-being, sanity, and relationships.

EXERCISE #2
ORIGINS OF MOMMY GUILT

For each of the five proximate reasons for mommy guilt, describe a situation with your child or children that elicited that response. Then, come up with strategies to replace those negative thoughts with positive actions. Reach out to close mom friends, if you can, for more perspective!

Aggression

_____

_____

_____

_____

Exit

_____

_____

_____

_____

Absence

_____

_____

_____

_____

Preferential treatment

_____

_____

_____

_____

Motherhood myth

_____

_____

_____

_____

CHAPTER 3

PERCEPTION IS REALITY: THE CONCEPT OF MINDSET

Mindset is an individual's set of beliefs and attitudes that predetermine his or her interpretation and response to life's situations, particularly challenges and difficulties. Dr. Carol S. Dweck, a professor of psychology at Stanford University, has written extensively about mindset and how mindset predicts achievement and success. In her mindset theory, she describes two types of mindsets: fixed and growth.

With a *fixed* mindset, an individual believes that certain traits like intelligence and talent are innate, immutable, and unchangeable. You either have "it" or you don't, so there is no need to work for success because success comes naturally. When you fail—and you will fail—you conclude that you do not possess the necessary raw talent and give up.

Those with a *growth* mindset believe those same traits can be honed and developed through the relationships they form and the opportunities they choose. They desire to learn and grow and view challenges as opportunities and failures as an indication to try again but in a different way. The focus is on mastery.

Dr. Dweck's mindset theory has major implications in several arenas including education, business, and, of course, parenting. As mothers, we often fall victim to a fixed mindset. We adopt unhealthy cognitions that negatively impact our parenting style and relationships with our children. We believe we parent ineffectively and that we will always struggle because we were raised in a single-parent household, because our parents argued viciously in front of us, because our parents had too many rules and used strict discipline, or because our parents did not practice healthy boundaries and gave us too much freedom.

We also think there is a "one size fits all" approach to motherhood, and either you do it right the first time or fail your children miserably. We catastrophize our bad decisions and conclude we will never be a good parent. Our children also suffer from our fixed mindset parenting style because, when we accept little responsibility for the mistakes we make, we internalize this belief. It be-

Adapted from Dr. Carol S. Dweck

Fixed Mindset   Growth Mindset

	Intelligence	
Innate, immutable, and unchangeable •		• Is honed and developed
Desire to appear smart •	**Primary Goals**	• Desire for mastery
Avoid challenges •	**Challenges**	• Embrace challenges
Become discouraged and give up •	**Failures**	• An opportunity to try something new
Taken personally, gets defensive •	**Criticism**	• Viewed as areas for improvement

Dr. Reesha

comes *"It's not my fault but rather the fault of my circumstances,"* so we see little need for improvement and no reason to try and make things better. We inadvertently pass this belief on to our children, and they adopt the same mentality.

Our past informs our present and future but certainly does not dictate them. We can grow, learn, and become better parents. We don't have to chastise ourselves when we choose unwisely. Tomorrow is a new day, another chance to make better decisions than you did yesterday. Maybe you yell at your children twice rather than five times. Maybe you laugh when your daughter insists on wearing the same outfit for the third day in a row rather than sigh loudly and angrily demand that she change her clothes.

I know this is easier said than done. As a child and adolescent psychiatrist, I used to think my training and expertise would prepare me for almost any parenting challenge that came my way. I always had an answer for moms who brought their children to see me in my clinic. One of my favorite words was "consistent." I often would say, "You just need to be consistent with so and so…" to derive the desired behavior from one's child. I said this with anything from sleep schedules and healthier eating habits to potty training and management of temper tantrums.

But I, too, struggled to put my own wise, doctorly advice into practice. When my oldest was only nine months old, she took her first trans-Atlantic flight. My husband was attending a track and field conference in Phoenix, Arizona, and Bailey and I were heading to meet him out there. I was excited, albeit nervous, since this was my first trip to Arizona, and with my baby girl no less. Still, I thought I was adequately prepared. I would nurse her during takeoff and landing, and she would sleep in between. If she fussed, I would read to her quietly.

Surprise, surprise: my plans didn't work. She nursed during takeoff and drifted off to sleep but woke up midway. She started getting fussy but none of my strategies to calm her down worked. She did not want to nurse again, bouncing her was useless, and reading did not soothe her. The seatbelt fasten sign was illuminated, so I couldn't get up and walk around with her. I started panicking because I didn't know what to do. I kept looking around, worried that another passenger was going to get upset at my fussy baby and her unprepared new momma.

Then, an angel appeared. A woman sitting nearby tapped me on my shoulder and handed me a little squeaky toy for Bailey. Bailey's attention shifted, and she quickly calmed down. I was relieved but then felt awful because I had not thought to bring any of her favorite toys with me on this trip. I quickly concluded that I was a bad mother—fixed mindset at work.

I learned then that one of the major tasks for eliminating mommy guilt was to shift my fixed mindset to a growth mindset. We must change our perspective on motherhood. There are clearly wrong ways to parent but thousands of good ways. Give yourself, other moms, and your children a healthy dose of grace. When you find yourself frustrated and overwhelmed, laugh until your cheeks hurt and your sides ache instead of exploding in anger. But forgive yourself if you do explode! Find three or four good parenting websites and books that really resonate with you and learn about major developmental tasks for your child by age and stage. Arm yourself with tips you can implement to make your morning routine easier or reduce dinner time struggles. Then, share what you learn with other moms. Be open to constructive feedback. It's not a personal attack on your character, and it might even be incredibly informative.

Most importantly, and I cannot reiterate this fact enough, forgive yourself when you falter and apologize to your children when you lose control or make the wrong choice. Our children are watching, and they model much more of what we say and do than we may realize. They need to see us have bad outcomes and keep pressing, so they won't give up when the same happens to them. They also need to hear our apologies when our anger gets the best of us, so they, too, can learn to apologize when they are in the wrong.

I would be remiss if I failed to mention the potential psychological consequences of unchecked mommy guilt. Parenting is hard work, and the impact of mothering and mommy guilt can be brutal. What may start as fatigue, frustration, and stress can lead to mood swings, irritability, and worry that begin to hit daily rather than episodically. The consequences affect not only ourselves but our families, children, work, and other relationships.

Moms may also develop depression or anxiety, two mental illnesses that are occur commonly in women. According to the Centers for Disease Control and Prevention (CDC), Major Depressive Disorder (MDD) affects one in ten women in the United States. Symptoms of depression include persistent sad mood, irritability, anhedonia (the inability to experience pleasure from activities that one usually finds enjoyable), social isolation and withdrawal, sleep changes (too much or too little sleep), appetite changes (overeating or loss of appetite), fatigue or loss of energy, lack of motivation, difficulty concentrating, indecisiveness, excessive and inappropriate guilt, feeling like a burden to others, worthless and hopeless feelings, and thoughts of suicide or suicidal ideation. Suicidal ideation can range from wishing that you don't wake up in the morning or hoping for a fatal accident, all the way to actively planning to take your life.

Postpartum depression (PPD) is depression that occurs after childbirth and affects one in nine American women. Symptoms of PPD are similar to those of MDD, but up to 50% of women with PPD go undiagnosed. Postpartum depression severely impairs a new mom's ability to take care of herself and her new baby. Anxiety is also common and may manifest as excessive worry, irritability, disrupted sleep, racing thoughts, tension headaches, and a nagging sense of dread. Some women may have full on panic attacks triggered by worry and stress. Classic symptoms of panic attacks include rapid heart rate, shortness of breath, sensation of choking, sweating, trembling or shaking, chest pressure or tightness, feeling dizzy or lightheaded, numbness or tingling in your hands or feet, fear of losing control, or belief that you are dying.

Suicidal thoughts are a medical emergency. Please seek help immediately if you or someone you know voices thoughts of suicide. Call a friend or family mem-

Symptoms of Depression

Thoughts of suicide

Depressed
or
irritable mood

Loss of interest
in pleasureable activities

Worthlessness

Changes in sleep

Difficulty concentrating

Fatigue,
loss of energy

Changes in appetite and weight

Dr. Reesha

ber, call 911, drive to the nearest emergency room, or call a hotline. The National Suicide Prevention Lifeline telephone number is 1-800-273-8255. Someone is available twenty-four hours a day, seven days a week. Never be ashamed or embarrassed to get the help you deserve. Your life depends on it.

EXERCISE #3
MINDSET SHIFTS

Moms, take a moment and reflect. Are you operating with a growth mindset or a fixed mindset? Are their certain situations when you find it harder to embrace a growth mindset?

To help mommies shift from a fixed to a growth mindset, I have crafted five Mommy Affirmations that we can all say daily.

1. I am enough.

2. I make mistakes, but tomorrow will be a better day.

3. There is no such thing as the perfect mommy and definitely no such thing as perfect kids.

4. I'm not in this parenting journey alone.

5. All mommies need a little help sometimes, and that's a good thing.

CHAPTER 4

LIES, LIES, AND MORE LIES: DISMANTLING PERVASIVE MOTHERHOOD MYTHS

*"Being a mother is learning about strengths
you didn't know you had and dealing with fears
you didn't know existed."*

—Linda Wooten

Whoever coined the phrase "You can have it all" must not have raised any children. Similar to this is the notion of work-life balance, a philosophy espoused by many. Admittedly, I have been on a quest for work-life balance since I had my first child in 2007. I searched for the "secret sauce," the answer to finding a balanced life. I bought a planner to better manage my time, I prioritized my responsibilities, I hired a nanny, and I found some time here and there for massages and facials, date nights with the hubby, and dinner with my girlfriends.

While I was attempting to "work smarter, not harder," I remained stressed and stretched, pulled in a million different directions. It seemed like every other mom I knew had it all together, but I was drowning, unable to keep my head above water. But with time and after two more kids, I stopped misconstruing my inability to balance my life as evidence of my ineptitude. What has helped me in that process is to have wonderfully transparent conversations with a core group of women I affectionately call "my tribe." We speak openly about the challenges of juggling multiple hats and ponder tough questions about marriage, parenting, and womanhood. We bring strategies and solutions for one another with compassion and a lot of laughter. We'll talk more about the importance of your mom tribe later in the chapter.

What I gleaned from my experiences and honest talks with my tribe is this: *work-life balance is an elusive myth*. The real balance comes from defining what you and your family need for that season in life and embracing the shifts and transitions as they come. In this season of my life, I am a Jesus-lover (and always will be), a wife, mother to three young children, full-time physician, budding entrepreneur, and rising author. Yes, I can have it all but just not all at one time. And that's okay! Frankly, it's liberating! There will be times when I pour much of my energy into my children and effective parenting with less emphasis on preparing home-cooked meals or reading the latest psychiatry journal. At other times, I will be on my A-game as a physician or wife but less focused on my children.

I shift my priorities daily or even more frequently to fit the need at the time, and I don't berate myself for not being superwoman. I give a total of 100% for the day, but not 100% for each task at hand. I no longer feel the need to strive for perfectionism or pretend like I have it all together. There is beauty and truth in my vulnerability; and without it, there is no growth, no transformation. Flexibility, grace, and humor comprise my secret sauce.

Like work-life balance, there are other lies that we perpetuate and those impressed upon us. We've all heard them before, catchphrases the we recite to ourselves and share with each other supposedly to motivate, inspire, and encourage. These sayings are supposed to be helpful when we feel overwhelmed and filled with doubt. But in all honesty, they aren't true. I'll share a few of these mistruths here, some of which apply generally to womanhood and others more specifically to parenting:

1. *You can have it all*: I discussed this concept earlier. The bottom line is, we can have it all, just not all in one day. The sum total of what we give should equal 100%, but we cannot give 100% daily to each individual part. I am woman, hear me roar, but even superheroes can't get it all done in one day.

2. *Beauty is only skin deep*: In an era where a woman's value is placed upon her youth, measurements, and physical appearance, the adage of "beauty is only skin deep" is hypocrisy. Women spend billions of dollars every year on makeup, skin care regimens, Botox, body sculpting procedures, and plastic surgery to achieve what many would argue is a very narrow ideal of beauty. Thankfully, there has been a recent trend in the media in which a more inclusive view of beauty features women of color, older women, and women falling outside of conventional size standards. Female celebrities post "makeup-free" images on their social media pages, and beauty campaigns now celebrate diversity.

    Indeed, a woman's outer appearance is no substitute for her character; however, your health is your wealth. While you need not focus on outer beauty that society deems attractive and desirable, you must pay attention to your overall health and well-being. This means adopting healthy eating habits, limiting your sugar and alcohol intake, engaging in regular exercise, practicing good self-care, and positively managing your stress. Outer beauty as a proxy for health and wellness is not all bad.

3. *The best things in life are free*: Big dreams, nighttime snuggles with my babies, and stolen kisses...yes, some of the best things in life are free. I also choose to celebrate the everyday beauty in life, practice gratitude, and serve others. Each of these actions I do freely as they fill my love bucket and remind me to count my blessings daily, to never forget the fragility of life.

   With that being said, some of the best experiences like travel and vacations, fly shoes, shopping, and incredible experiences for my children cost money. I work hard and sacrifice so that I can play harder and fully enjoy all that this life has to offer.

4. *Good things come to those who wait*: Merriam-Webster's dictionary defines "wait" as "to stay in a place until an expected event happens" or "to

remain in a state in which you expect or hope that something will happen soon." Waiting requires patience but lacks initiative. There is no movement, no momentum. So, how will good things come without action? In this day and age, I ascribe to the mindset of grabbing the bull by the horns. If I want something or desire a change, waiting will only leave me stuck and in expectation. If I pursue my dreams through a series of calculated steps grounded in discipline, commitment, and preparation, then I can achieve my goals.

You now have a new perspective on commonly used phrases and ideologies. However, like I mentioned earlier, the key to dismantling myths and surviving motherhood is your tribe, a community of women who center you, encourage you, push you, uphold you, and uplift you. My tribe is everything. My girls pray for and with me. They love my children and root for my marriage.

Mommas, we all need a rock star tribe. The mothers in my crew display certain character traits, each of which tremendously benefit me, personally and professionally. I urge you to surround yourself with similar women and watch how much progress you will make encircled by other amazing mommas.

1. *The sagely momma:* This thoughtful and discerning friend is often more seasoned by her age, the number and ages of her children, her experiences, or her career and professional expertise. She gives practical advice and is an all-around wonderful resource.

2. *The "keep it real" momma:* She rarely tell us what we want to hear but always tells us what we need to hear. No fluff or warm and fuzzy anecdotes here! She brings the raw, unadulterated truth.

3. *The comedian momma:* She is the friend who brings much-needed comic relief. Whether you are on the verge of bursting into tears because you can't take anymore pee puddles on the floor, toys stuffed down the toilet, attitude from your ten-year-old daughter who ain't even hit puberty, or arguments with your hubby, she has something for you. A masterful storyteller, this momma shares tales that will have you laughing so hard your cheeks hurt.

4. *Spiritually-grounded momma:* She centers and refocuses your energies. Faith is an essential component for many moms; but amid all the busyness and chaos that is life, we can get bogged down and disconnected. This mama provides a

gentle reminder that the world is bigger than you and that you exist for a much greater purpose. She brings scripture, prayer, or meditation and lovingly reframes our perspective.

Ladies, I encourage you to find your tribe. With these women, you can share amazing times and get through the difficult and painful ones. When you find these precious relationships, cherish them. Hold them close to your heart.

EXERCISE #4
SQUAD GOALS

Who's in your tribe? Think about four or five of your closest friends and the roles they play in your life. Jot their names and roles down. Which key player is missing?

CHAPTER 5

A NEW PARADIGM SHIFT: LEARNING TO DITCH THE MOMMY GUILT

"There is no way to be a perfect mother, and a million ways to be a good one."

—Jill Churchill

Since we now know how to recognize mommy guilt and can acknowledge that we've all likely experienced it to some degree, let's explore strategies to successfully conquer the guilt. We all want what's best for our children but no longer at our expense. In this chapter, we will learn to accept ourselves for who we are and figure out the best ways to support each other and our families in our own unique and individual ways.

1. ONE SIZE DOES NOT FIT ALL

Families are as diverse as the parents and children that make them up. We bring our own personality traits, strengths and weaknesses, gifts and talents, preferences, hang-ups, and biases. Those similarities and differences define the core of our identity and make our lives and relationships rich, interesting, and unexpected. So, to think that one broadly applicable parenting strategy would work for all children and families is an outrageous idea.

Still, we often search for that one great tool or resource that will ensure success. While such resources can be enormously helpful, the only tactic that I know to work for *all* families and in *all* situations is flexibility. Merriam-Webster's dictionary defines "flexibility" as a "ready capability to adapt to new, different, or changing requirements." That spells parenting to a tee. As our children grow and develop, they transform physically, cognitively, emotionally, socially, morally, and spiritually. Their needs, especially what they require from their parents, change.

As parents, flexibility helps us view our children's choices and desires from a developmental framework rather than simply as right or wrong. We can employ disciplinary techniques that emphasize their natural gifts rather than those that magnify their shortcomings.

My pint-sized toddler is in the midst of her "threenage" year, and I find her simultaneously irresistibly adorable and incredibly frustrating. Daily she insists on asserting her independence, communicating her emotions, and demonstrating mastery of her growing vocabulary. I get everything from "I can do it" to "Mommy, I'm getting mad at you" to pulling out one of her children's book and "reading me a story" using all kinds of big words for a three-year-old. These tasks are critical at this developmental stage, so I let her feed herself and dress herself, even when she makes a huge mess that I have to clean up or when she dresses inappropriately for the season. I laugh instead of feeling exasperated because her demands make sense. My older two children are at different developmental stages that necessitate something completely different.

I also consider other characteristics unique to my family when deciding how to proceed with major decisions such as the ages of my children, our work schedule, and the presence or absence of extended family. We do what works for the Cox family of five, which may or may not work as well for the Brinkley family of three.

2. STOP COMPARING

Why are we trying to keep up with the Joneses anyway? Once you up your game, another set of Joneses come along with bigger and better stuff. Furthermore, we draw inferences by looking at the external and use that to inform our perception of the internal. The problem is that our perception is usually off-base, if not flat-out wrong. The mom you see in the grocery store allowing her two-year-old to scream loudly all while wearing the messy bun and no makeup might not be a hot mess. She might just be having a hard day or even received devastating news, but you've already sized her up and decided she is simply too overwhelmed. And what about the slender, well-dressed mommy donning Christian Louboutin's? You may aspire to be like her, but she may be fashioning a beautiful outer appearance to hide the pain and despair of a crumbling marriage.

Many times, we moms share similar struggles; but just as often, those challenges are uniquely our own. Don't minimize her difficulties or vilify her strengths because they seem less problematic than yours. She may come from money or have only one kid to your four, but she is still human and her struggles and emotions are real and valid. Socioculturally, we live in an era where women are sexualized, told they are beautiful only if they are young and slender, are criticized when their bodies grow a little rounder from having children, and made to feel less than if she chooses career over family. We may snap back at these gendered stereotypes; but we, too, often unwittingly judge and compare our own cohort in vicious cycles. We moms must champion each other and stop the gossip and harsh criticism.

3. SAY "NO" TO PERFECTIONISM

There are no perfect kids and no perfect parents. Perfectionism is nothing to which to aspire. Even pediatrician-turned-child psychoanalyst Dr. Donald Winnicott coined the term "good enough mothering" to speak to the tension between selflessly caring for a child while balancing a mother's own needs and desires so that the two goals are reconciled without harming the baby.

Remember, we don't have to be perfect and we *will* fail repeatedly. Those facts do not constitute bad parenting. More importantly, when we do fail, we need to apologize to our children for our missteps, continue to love them fiercely, vow to try and do better, and then do it all over again. Our children learn most, not when we are doing everything right but when we face adversity and seemingly insurmountable challenges. They grow when we demonstrate our faith and tenacity and the power of the human spirit.

4. MOMMY-ING IS HARD WORK

I don't care what anyone says: parenting is not easy, it does not always come naturally, and moms most certainly do not enjoy parenting every single day. Some days I don't want to be anybody's momma! The adage says that the days are long and the years are short, but right now, all I see are long, long days. Sometimes, I feel taken for granted, disrespected, and devalued by my three little ones. No one seems to care about my feelings or my day at work. My request for a few moments to sit quietly is met with a barrage of questions and demands. I fight the urge not to mutate into a three-headed monster as the words "Did you not just hear me?" roar through me.

This is normal because this is human. Do not punish yourself for having real feelings, and do not be afraid to talk about them openly.

5. CHOOSE TO FOCUS MORE ON THE JOYS AND LESS ON THE CHALLENGES OF PARENTING

Whether you have one child or four, you stay at home or work outside the home, or you function as a single parent or co-parent with your significant other, we all wrestle with the busyness that is motherhood every single day. We lament sleepless nights, the terrible two's and three's, potty training, and the endless juggling of extracurricular activities. We commiserate with other moms about sullen teenagers and how to prepare our children for college and adulthood. We police social media accounts and wonder if we should drug-test our children. The list of worries and challenges seem never-ending.

Instead of focusing on the difficulties that come along with parenting, focus on the joys of raising your child. One day, he will not want to snuggle and cuddle, and she won't run to you first after a fight with her best friend. Take time every day to intentionally cherish the wonderful aspects of parenting. Delight in those first moments: first smile, first crawl, first steps, first words, first boo-boo you kiss, first birthday, first Christmas, first "I love you, mommy," first dress-shopping for a school dance, first driver's license and first car, first college tour.

Remember all the hopes and dreams you have for your children. Ponder the all-consuming love that is so vast that your heart swells to the point of bursting at the mere thought of them. Those memories pull us through the darkest of days when we fail more than we try and cry out of frustration or even despair. Press those memories into the deep recesses of your brain like a weathered book whose well-worn pages you will thumb through someday in the future.

6. SELF-CARE MAKES YOU A BETTER MOMMY

Self-care is critical to a mom's ability to manage the highs and lows of parenting. One of my favorite strategies is to schedule time for myself daily. Now, what that looks like on a day-to-day basis will differ depending on what's going on in my life. On a hectic day, I might take fifteen minutes to pray/meditate or read a magazine article. I might opt for a facial and massage, dinner with my girlfriends, or a date night with my husband when I have a bit more time.

I found an eye-opening blog post by Brianna Weist who enlightened my perspective on self-care. In her November 2017 blog post entitled, "This is What Self-

Care REALLY Means, because It's Not All Salt Baths and Chocolate Cake," Weist writes, "[T]rue self-care … is making the choice to not build a life you don't need to regularly escape from."[3] For moms, this means to live within your means rather than trying to keep up with the Joneses. Or perhaps it means to choose one extra-curricular activity per child instead of two or three and to require quiet time for everybody in the house. Self-care also means saying "no" to things you don't want to do, can't really do, or would overextend you. Take care of yourself, then you will be better equipped to be a better mommy.

7. YOU EXIST OUTSIDE OF YOUR ROLE AS A MOTHER

We moms tend to emphasize parenting as our life's work and believe that our children are our greatest contribution to the world. But we existed before we were moms. We had a life, we had dreams, we had desires, and we had goals and ambitions. Our role as a mother does not define our identity and self-worth. When your children grow up and leave home, you still need to know who you are, develop and maintain friendships, and enjoy hobbies. Don't forget who you are and the things that are important to you just because you are raising children.

8. YOUR LIFE DOES NOT AND SHOULD NOT REVOLVE AROUND YOUR CHILDREN

My three children are top priorities in my life, but by no means are they my only priority. In the mornings, Bailey, Evan, and Khloe must get ready for school, but no one is going anywhere if mommy does not shower and get dressed, make sure lunches are packed and book bags are ready at the door, and prepare breakfast. Similarly, at night, no one gets put to bed until mommy cooks dinner, bathes three children, and reads bedtime stories. There are no family vacations or extra purchases at Target unless mommy and daddy get up and go to work every day.

My children can't always be my #1 priority, and helping them understand this fact is a good thing. Truthfully, it is essential to their emotional development. Who better to teach them that the world does not revolve around them than their loving parents? Our kids must know that, sometimes, there are other, more pressing issues than their own needs. They must learn to wait without always complaining, exercise patience, and self-soothe when they are disappointed. Yes, they must learn to be grateful for second or even third place, because no one always wins. We successfully prepare our children for adulthood when we practice these important life lessons.

9. THE AMOUNT OF TIME SPENT WITH OUR CHILDREN IS NOT AS CRITICAL AS WE THINK

Many of us moms might have partaken in or have even fallen victim to the epic battle that rages between moms who work and those who stay at home. Society often tells us that moms who stay at home are better because they spend almost every waking moment with their children, satisfying their every need and demand. After all, stay-at-home moms choose children over careers, uninterrupted time over early mornings departures and late-night meetings, home-cooked meals over fast food dinners, and their child's well-being over their own. Or that's what society tells us they should do.

In actuality, research shows that more time with our children *does not* lead to better outcomes. A 2015 study by Melissa A. Milkie, et al.[4] found that the amount of maternal time (simply present or actively engaged) spent with children between ages three to eleven had no deleterious effects on their emotional health, behaviors, or academic performance. What did matter and positively or negatively impacts outcomes for children were factors termed "social status resources," which include things like mom's education level, household income, and traditional family structure (married biological parents vs. single-parent households or blended families). For adolescents, the findings were similar. In the end, the amount of time was not the issue but rather the quality of the time spent. Even if a mother spent only a little time with her children, as long as that time was spent engaged in activities together, it reduced delinquent behavior (sex, drugs, poor peer choices).

There is always a choice for moms. Moms choose what works best for their families. We must respect each other's decisions as we ask for them to respect ours. Why war with each other when we can support each other?

10. FEELINGS AIN'T FACTS

Sometimes, we get confused. We believe that how we feel about a situation constitutes the pure, unadulterated truth. While feelings are *our* truth, these emotions do not represent *The Truth*.

You may feel like a bad mom. You may feel like you will never lose the baby weight. You may think that you failed your child because you lost control of your anger.

You may think no one will ever hire you again because you stayed out of the work force for ten years to raise your children. These are your feelings, your beliefs, and your thoughts; but just because they are yours does not make them accurate. Feelings are not facts!

11. GET HELP BEFORE YOU BECOME UTTERLY OVERWHELMED

Parenting skills are not ingrained just because we are women. We hire financial planners to help us manage our money, a hair stylist to color and cut our hair, and personal trainers and nutritionists to transform our bodies. Why not take parenting classes, view a parenting webinar, or join a parent support group to learn how to parent more effectively? Why not talk to your pediatrician, read a few books, check out a parenting blog, or hire a parenting coach?

Asking for help takes courage—much more courage than continuing to struggle and feeling like a failure. We are not meant to go through life alone; rather, we are meant to do life through relationships with others. No mom needs to sink under the weight of negativity. Reach out to your tribe, your throng of women who nurture you and hold you accountable. These are the women who speak life-giving and life-affirming words and encourage you to get help when you need it. It's hard work, mommas, and we all need help sometimes.

EXERCISE #5

Pick three parenting hang-ups with which you are currently struggling and write them down here. After each hang up, come up with three actionable steps you can take to negate these erroneous ways of thinking.

A. _____

1. _____

2. _____

3. _____

B. _____

1. _____

2. _____

3. _____

C. _____

1. _____

2. _____

3. _____

CHAPTER 6

GUILT-FREE PARENTING: REFLECTIONS ON SELF-CARE, RESILIENCE, AND OTHER LESSONS FOR OUR CHILDREN

"Motherhood has a very humanizing effect. Everything gets reduced to essentials."

—Meryl Streep

We hear stories of families who have faced incredible obstacles, some from our close-knit circle of friends or our own families. I have two stories—one from the Bragg family and another from my dear friend Wynell "Wyndy" Gilbert, both from Birmingham, Alabama, that highlight beauty, fortitude, and most of all, resilience.

In 2016, Clara Bragg was diagnosed with Late Infantile GM1 Gangliosidosis. Also known as beta-galactosidase 1 deficiency, this inherited lysosomal storage disorder progressively destroys nerve cells or neurons in the brain and spinal cord. A lysosome is a specialized part of an animal cell that breaks down different types of biological molecules. In Late Infantile GM1 Gangliosidosis, a mutation in the GLB1 gene prevents an enzyme called beta-galactosidase from breaking down GM1 ganglioside, which leads to a toxic accumulation of this protein in the body.

When diagnosed with Late Infantile GM 1 Gangliosidosis, a child will experience loss of developmental milestones, seizures, an enlarged liver and spleen, muscle weakness, gait (walking) disturbance, and skeletal changes. Children with this devastating neurological condition typically do not survive past early childhood.

After Clara received this heart-breaking diagnosis, her parents sprang into action, choosing to do something inspiring. Instead of being paralyzed by grief in the face of unimaginable circumstances, Clara's parents decided to form a fundraising campaign aptly named A Cure for Clara. Through this organization, they host events and fundraisers to raise money to support research efforts for the Cure GM1 Foundation.

An educator for over fifteen years, Wynell "Wyndy" Gilbert suddenly found herself looking for another job when her teaching contract was not renewed. Angry and disappointed, she questioned the school's decision. Then she began a process of careful and honest introspection. Did she deserve this cut? Had she inadvertently taken some missteps or made a fatal error unbeknownst to her? Had she lost her passion for teaching? Was her true purpose leading her elsewhere?

She spent time pondering these questions, sought counsel from friends and colleagues, and began to pray and earnestly seek God for His guidance. Birthed from this difficult trial was a tremendous gift, the creation of her new business, WKG Educational Consulting, LLC, a boutique consulting firm that specializes in providing the highest level of academic support to parents, schools, and educators. Rather than allow an unexpected job loss to derail her purpose, Wyndy used her termination as an opportunity to design a service that uniquely pairs her talents and skills to meet the educational needs of a community of children and families.

Resilience is a term that describes an individual's capacity to adapt and thrive in the face of stress, challenges, trauma, and adversity. Resilience falls on a spectrum from minimally to highly resilient; but thankfully, this is not a skill you either have or you don't. Resilience can be cultivated and nurtured.

People who have minimal resilience tend to view themselves as the victim, are more prone to mood instability, fatigue, and distress. They adopt an external locus of control wherein they believe things happen to them, thus things are always completely outside of their control. They often have poor coping skills and are at higher risk for mood and anxiety disorders. Those with higher resilience can pull from an emotional reserve, if you will.

Let's think of resilience in terms of a bank where you hold both checking and savings accounts. Your checking account is what you use for your day-to-day purchases and expenditures, and you maintain steady employment to fund your checking account. Most of the time, you can manage your needs and some of your wants from your checking account.

On the other hand, you have money in your savings account for emergencies like car or home repairs. If you don't make extra deposits into your savings account, you won't have the money to pay for those unexpected costs. Well, resilience is your emotional savings account.

Most of us have some ability to manage day-to-day life situations with our regular emotional resources. However, when adverse events or all-out crises like divorce, illness, trauma, or death of loved ones occur, we find ourselves ill-equipped because our emotional banks are inadequately funded. Without that backup resource, we are left fatigued, unable to sleep or sleeping too much, irritable, and unproductive. And if we continue to attempt to withdraw from an already overdrawn account, we are emptied and end up in the negative.

As moms, resilience is vital to our health and well-being. We are better parents, wives, friends, and co-workers when we possess the tools to weather the storms and unpredictability that life and parenting bring. We must also model and teach our children resilience, so they are prepared to triumphantly enter and exit the various developmental stages of childhood, adolescence, and adulthood.

Here are ten strategies to help you fill your emotional savings account and build your resilience:

1. *Practice gratitude*: Find joy in the everyday, in the mundane. From the moment you wake up, be grateful because someone did not have the opportunity to awaken today. As you drive to work

in a car you can afford to a job that pays your bills, be grateful. When your children repeatedly scream your name, be grateful—there are women all over the world who would give anything to be called "mommy." Focus less on what you don't have and what isn't going right and more on the good in your life.

2. *Cultivate mindfulness*: Mindfulness is the practice of being in the moment and fully present in the here and now—the opposite of busyness and multitasking, behaviors to which all moms succumb. Mindfulness must be cultivated especially during the times you are feeling defeated, irritable, or angry.

   Take a moment and sit. Close your eyes if you feel more comfortable. Relax your body. Focus on the firmness or softness of your chair. Notice the presence or absence of sound and the lighting. Attend to your breathing and then start to slow your breaths. Begin with a deep inhalation through your nose, then briefly hold your breath before exhaling deeply through your mouth.

   If your mind starts to wander during this exercise, refocus your attention on your breathing. Go through this cycle for a couple of minutes until you feel more relaxed and calm. Practice mindfulness daily.

3. *Prayer and meditation:* As a Christian woman, my faith is the cornerstone of my very being. My faith is the foundation upon which I have built my life, my family, and my career. I have go-to scriptures embroidered on my heart, upon which I rely in times of turmoil:

The Lord will guide you continually, giving you water when you are dry and restoring your strength. You will be like a well-watered garden, like an ever-flowing spring.

— Isaiah 58:11 NLT

The Lord will fight for you; you need only to be still.

— Exodus 14:14 NIV

The faithful love of the Lord never ends! His mercies never cease.

— Lamentations 3:22 NLT

Blessed is she who has believed that the Lord would fulfill His promises to her!

— Luke 1:45 NIV

Give all your worries and cares to God, for He cares about you.

—1 Peter 5:7 NLT

Prayer and my faith remind me that this life is not all about me. As a believer, I know that my God is greater than any problems I might face and that knowledge propels me to see beyond my immediate circumstances and challenges to a more hopeful time to come.

4. *Show kindness*: Kindness fills my love bucket. Whether it's a simple "hello" and a genuine smile or a stranger who holds the door open for me or who helps me clean up the mess my three-year-old made on Aisle 7, my heart swells when I am on the receiving end of random acts of kindness. In return, I show kindness to my loved ones, acquaintances, and strangers.

I challenge you to do something kind for someone every day, even when you, yourself, are struggling. You never know how a small display of kindness could turn someone's day completely around for the better, including yours.

5. *Exercise:* The physical health benefits of exercise are well-known, but there are multiple psychological benefits as well: increased endorphin levels (endorphins are brain chemicals that create feelings of euphoria), decreased stress and anxiety, improved memory and cognition, improved sleep, and boosts to self-esteem and self-confidence. According to the American College of Sports Medicine, adults should get at least 150 minutes of moderate-intensity exercise each week. This 150-minute goal can be divided into 30-minute sessions five days a week or three 60-minute blocks and should include both cardiovascular exercise and resistance training.

    Head to the gym, join a Pilates or CrossFit class, or run in your neighborhood with a few friends. Involve your children too—go on nature walks or challenge them to a Beyoncé-themed dance off. I mean, who doesn't love Beyoncé?

6. *Celebrate small victories:* When I work with children and families struggling with disruptive be-

havior, one of the first recommendations I make is to implement a strategy called "catch your child doing good." With this technique, parents catch their child in the act of a desired behavior instead of only when they are misbehaving. I instruct parents to find any behavior, no matter how small, for which to praise their child.

By the same token, we mommas need to celebrate our own victories, no matter how small. When I don't yell during the mad morning rush, I pat myself on the back. When my husband calls to asks me about what's on tonight's dinner menu and I actually know the answer, I praise myself. When I make it to the gym even one day out of the entire month, I play crunk music, dance in the mirror, and remind myself how cute I am. I celebrate every opportunity I get to feed the positive.

7. *The power of community and connection:* Surround yourself with positive people. Much like the women in your close-knit tribe, find people who uplift you, encourage you, and pour into you. Place men and women in your circle who challenge you to live better and parent better but without harsh words and demoralizing judgments.

8. *Accept that change and adversity are inevitable:* No matter where you were born and raised, who your parents are, to whom you are married, or how much money you make, you will face triumphs and disappointments. Life, despite your best efforts to plan and prepare, will be unpredictable and difficult at times. Expected and unexpected changes will come. Don't ignore this inevitable reality; instead, anticipate and accept it.

9. *Unplug and disengage:* This era of Facebook, Instagram, Twitter, and Snapchat brings unique dimensions to interpersonal relationships and communication; however, lack of privacy, false realities, and trends towards immediate gratification are problematic. There is far too much negativity, racism, sexism, and Internet-trolling that goes on these days. If we allow it, our newsfeed will remain inundated with offensive material that pushes us into a funky, disagreeable headspace. With your daily exercise schedule, four-hour-long meal-planning Sundays, weekly book club meetings, and the kids' extracurricular activities, all that online negativity may be the straw that breaks the camel's back. Sometimes, we just need to unplug from technology and the

busyness of the week and take a little me-time without all the extras.

10. *Reframe your perspective:* Many of us catastrophize in the midst of a crisis. We anticipate the worst, which informs how we respond to stressful events. If we expect the worse, we are less apt to rely on healthy coping skills and more likely to employ a "fight or flight" response, which can be detrimental to our mental health. Be hopeful and envision the positive. A positive attitude sets the tone and shifts our expectation towards a more favorable outcome.

Develop these skills to foster resilience and pass them on to your children!

THANK YOU

Thank you to all the mommies who want more and have the desire to ditch the mommy guilt. I applaud you for deciding to intentionally shift your mindset from one of guilt and shame to one of courage, acceptance, and growth. You are enough!

Follow me on Facebook at drleeshapsych and on Twitter & Instagram @drleesha.

Check out my website and blog at www.drleesha.com

REFERENCES

1. Pew Research Center (2007). Motherhood Today: Tougher Challenges, Less Success. Retrieved from http://www.pewsocialtrends.org/2007/05/02/motherhood-today-tougher-challenges-less-success/.

2. Rotkirch, A., and K. Janhunen (2009). Maternal Guilt. *Evolutionary Psychology*, 8(1): 90–106.

3. Weist, B. "This is What 'Self-Care' REALLY Means, Because It's Not all Salt Baths and Chocolate Cake." Retrieved from https://thoughtcatalog.com/brianna-wiest/2017/11/this-is-what-self-care-really-means-because-its-not-all-salt-baths-and-chocolate-cake/ (accessed December 4, 2017).

4. Milkie, M. A., Monaguchi, K. M., Denny K.E. (2015). Does the Amount of Time Mothers Spend With Children or Adolescents Matter? *Journal of Marriage and Family*, 77: 355–372.

ABOUT THE AUTHOR

Leesha M. Ellis-Cox, MD, MPH, is a board-certified child, adolescent, and adult psychiatrist, public speaker, author, wife, mother, and woman of God. In addition to her work as a full-time physician, she is a leading authority on women's and children's mental health and serves as a highly sought-after parenting expert, especially for mothers struggling with "mommy guilt." She is a recipient of the Alabama Department of Mental Health's RE-SPECT award; and in her spare time, she volunteers her services at the Worship Center Christian Church in Birmingham, Alabama.

Dr. Ellis-Cox earned her medical degree from the University of North Carolina (UNC) at Chapel Hill. She completed her general psychiatry residency training at Emory University School of Medicine in Atlanta, followed by a joint fellowship in child and adolescent psychiatry and community psychiatry/public health, during which she obtained her Master of Public Health. She resides in the Birmingham area with her husband and their three children.

To learn more, visit her website at www.drleesha.com

CREATING DISTINCTIVE BOOKS
WITH INTENTIONAL RESULTS

We're a collaborative group of creative masterminds
with a mission to produce high-quality books to position
you for monumental success in the marketplace.

Our professional team of writers, editors, designers,
and marketing strategists work closely together to ensure
that every detail of your book is a clear representation
of the message in your writing.

Want to know more?
Write to us at info@publishyourgift.com
or call (888) 949-6228

Discover great books, exclusive offers, and more at
www.PublishYourGift.com

Connect with us on social media

@publishyourgift